SIGNS OF LIFE

JOHN GIERACH

CHERRY VALLEY EDITIONS

Publication credits: *The Coldspring Journal; THE 14; Bombay Gin; Mr. Cogito*

Cover photo: Gil Lipp

Library of Congress Cataloging in Publication Data
Gierach, John, 1946-
    Signs of life.

    Poems.
    I. Title.
PS3557.126S5   811'.5'4   77-21791
ISBN 0-916156-26-5

Typeset by Ed Hogan/Aspect Composition,
66 Rogers Ave., Somerville, Mass. 02144

for Carol

*We must talk now. I am no longer sure of the words,
the clockwork of the world. What is inexplicable*

Is the 'preponderance of objects'

George Oppen

SIGNS OF LIFE

seeing Reed and Charley on the roof today
I left the truck for a minute of talk
swedish ivy, Robert Creeley etc.
meanwhile life in general cools to a scum
that requires constant stirring
like instant coffee

scattered cars on the hot country road
little pieces of candy in a panic
the landlord floats by the shop window
alive and green
he crosses Harrison Avenue
and enters the church

typing late into thursday night
while Carol watches television
I go in there for a cigarette
see she is asleep
creep out
to smoke
think of
herons, ice, the St. Vrain River
dogs orbit the tree where the squirrel hides
light sticks like snow
making life dance on a black thing, a yellow thing and so on

Edison Engle once asked me
if I still meant what I'd said the day before
this is where the phrase "trojan horse votes"
comes from
and I thought of it just now
finishing the last of the crown royal
brain buzzing from lack of thought
solitary EXIT sign beaming through
locked school doors across Baseline

A Man Without God Is Like A Fish Without His Bicycle

Bob Fortner turns off the Husky station
this is a sign
no cigarettes till morning
"on some machines a piece will
slop over for no reason"
and in this I find hope
we can just roll on merrily
questions of God and Wrong being
tiresome in the hot humid air
at the Oxford Hotel

It was the time of dried things,
of the wheat-beard in the eye, and the flattened cat
of rusting iron on the giant bridges
and the absolute silence of cork

Lorca

I hear little kitchen sounds
Carol stuffing chilies with cheeze
night and autumn press their big hands on the window
they talk together
grow to immense size together

the great horned owls are exactly like themselves
generation to generation with no change
it's this that gives them their magic more than flight

the cats sit on the bed like hills on the moon
there was a feeling I used to get
hunting with my father and uncles
the edge of
the end of
the world every second

I stand in the doorway with the last cup of coffee
and watch the horse show across the road
it's the way the cops can ruin even death
with sheets and red lights
and the thought that in a better time
you could be around when the great mystery
turned inside out

the eviction notice throws a square shadow in the twilight
if my life wasn't like this
I wouldn't be writing poems
I don't have that many opinions

5:30 a.m. I almost vomit touching the cold wine bottle
from last night
it's either sentimentality or just
the sweetness of the last days of anything

well, are we gonna have a drink or should I
put on the coffee
I got so busy that
people got insistent and raw sewage
seeped into one of the wonders of the world

we were all living in this communal haze where
my pliers are your pliers and so
my tools were disappearing

Dave kicks the dog
and puts the cat back on the bed
we all slept till eleven & his starling died
our forefathers were better at this

if I read CATSKILL DIARY
instead of Meister Eckehart
it's because fish are more solid than theology

there were layers of mountains
above the old neighborhood
in the hard nights of late May
the women, being closer to life, had children
the men fought, the police came

I smoke Marlboros/Pall Mall extra lights
trying to get into something
with a filter

running water in the hot pan
the heat comes off
in a single wave
piling up
is one of the dangers of living
the yellow curbs get dirty
soon you can't tell
if you should park there or not

Charley George;
I've lost a lot of magic since February
I'm really freaked out
the variations of light
gives Le Bar a shimmer, a depth
25 maybe 30 people
and the details of *Jack's* life
a tapestry
something else spellbinding
money/the coming of winter
the waving black shadow of the elm in the yard
all afternoon
and into the night

there's another funeral at the Baptist church
the phone at the gas station rings and rings
my white tea cup and cigarette
on the white banister
look like a hospital
the church itself is white

Signs of Life

the gray cat
so absolute in "coldness"
does her (his) dance
out of pure economy
I take
as a sign of life

Jack Collom

1

at 3 in the morning
wide open time in the streets. . .
maybe an owl
or the fields
something we think of as huge

houses shrink in the hedges
there's always a dog barking
a hot car winding up miles away
signs of life, movement
something basic

2

"consciousness" might involve
the sifting out of memory
I'm waiting to recall these days fondly
there's a flash of it
a sliver of green light
waiting at Public Road

3

the Rolling Stones get blacker, richer
the less I work the more money I need
but the strain is something

life
stories
bummers
maybe a book

4

and the cars
the pretty compacts
that foretell a new age
the great roar gets a little tinny

5

storming in the kitchen
getting a little mad before work
a plume of black smoke to the left of the cat in the window
& the school busses who,
because they haul the children,
think they can do no wrong

6

war news;
once again the farmers manage
to kill a few tanks
Carol sweating in dreamland
and the "lateness of the hour"
seem to have some bearing
silence
that is
nothing obvious

7

hailstones
after coffee and a few words in the kitchen
the spots are gone but it's wet

and then it's dark
a fact of physics
(all the sciences)
the ground shines in the streetlight
there are no possessions
that someone with the right credentials
or age
loss etc.
can't take away
moment to moment like a blackbird

it's a way of bleeding
five hundred and ninety two things
costing a dollar and a half apiece

I don't have the exact figures

(sliding into night
chili rellenos
budweiser
naropa
duende)
a bicyclist rides through town and the dogs barking
like a wave
a shudder
eight o'clock
supper is ready

rain falls for the third night
mountains above the city
lie in a great fog space
at their best
like a woman
the furnace sings a song of new life
after a long summer

cicadas fall silent
snow falls above 9 thousand feet
the kitchen door swells and won't close
then won't open

October,
we who whisper "kitty kitty kitty"
in the dead of night
salute you

today I drove past a vacant lot where a year ago
stood the house of a woman I met at a party
and went to see but she wasn't home
and I felt the same loss again
only October
the trees aren't black
nor the fields white enough

the fat moon is there again
geese flying past the brick chimneys
at Public Service and all the lights coming on
it's not night
it's not night yet

this winter at the mercy of the arabs and the elements
the world's full of trouble
& the black rain in the streets
the radio says turns to snow
then rice
then wisdom

how many good nights has love ruined?
I mean the little sounds we take
for silence in town
easy hardship
snow flashing at 5 degrees
and the dirty barges on the river
hauling the fire and the light

the cottonwoods at the Baptist church jump in the wind
I can hear pancakes

the junipers at the cemetery throb like
36 green hearts
iron blue sky
empty school
the streets deserted as if there were some danger
some new law

Borges' laugh is so kind perhaps
ambition should be put aside
I make breakfast, go to work
green fronds of mucus on the sidewalk

67
nearly spring
"you like to play basketball?
"ya? well ah I HAVE a basketball...
one poet sits down another
prepares to read
some relief of tension, he leaves the podium for a minute
as more coffee is ordered
life itself is like this

days of fog
the vegetable world swells up
a new madness for every difference
fiddling with the sweetness of coffee
adjusting it downward over a period of weeks
as though systematically removing the love from marriage
in order to relax and live longer

sitting at the kitchen table
a transformer humming in the alley
and the mature rubble of life
2 big canadas and 3 vomit colored goslings
on the lake

home alone

I know you read everything on the typewriter
from beyond the door comes the song of the dog
a moment
before I finally open up
there is enough brilliance left over to read by
that's how it works for me
the duck call, the goose call and the squirrel

air moves
or we move through it
like in cars
beyond that nothing
a still life
motorcycle
white sky
an owl slicing the cold air
of a small city.
think of someone at home
asleep
while you have to ride the god damn train
farmers stand up in the fog
the iron in the hills
the wind on the rivers

looking for the bindery
crossing the Platte again and again
deep in thought
as if when one thing clicks
so does another and so on
brown snow yellow sky

the sound of Johns' phone ringing in his empty apartment
the undersides of willow leaves in the wind
sniper fire and rocket exchanges between Christians and Muslims
the pretty trees in the wilderness

it reads well
buying this and then
something else
it's a kind of resignation
I stumble a little and the coffee licks my hand

taking the dogs along to get the pizza
made it very homey
but there's this cuteness
I worry about
my arm doesn't have a lot of
grap
gristle
you know
the greyness of work
eating the white hills

my heart was singing
the broken pieces of tile were ground to powder
between the desk and the kitchen
it's something to endure
rabbits
and a few dollars
why are you being
a pain in the ass
at such a moment?

night is stupendous
in america, with so much behind us
we can't throw our hair into the void in the daylight
some can only think clearly while
driving, full of coffee, in the rain
maybe the gas gauge is on empty. . .
getting used to
a flick of night bird in the headlights

I was thinking about
walking out this morning into a green warm flush
the modes we invent;
poet and sportsman
avant guard punk
a trucker from Johnson's Corner writes
god help these wierdos

The Sadness In the Fields

in the cool Mexican alleys thinking
no one will visit us out here
there are two pay phones
the first one is broken

stop and get a beer

better, there's some lightening
the town is flat
hardwood
black hair
bug buzzing in circle on back

each cat takes a window and watches

living with Carol, strange toasters and honey
the agreement is anything anybody wants but
not at home
I pull the neighbor dog's tail
until it demonstrates submission
it is black white brown and small

Carol pats the calico
I type
drink Budweiser smoke type some more
and it goes nowhere
but any of these cars I hear could be John
(very quiet after the siren)
John comes we drink, talk and he leaves

in the fall the trees in town will be surpassed only
by the sadness in the fields
terrible chicano choppers
and the horror of lives lived on every side

tomorrow I will find the bar where
the caucasians hang out
the stillness
the long streets down which
the fields lie

taking the coffee off the strange new electric stove
there are small carbon fires
and the night is getting blue
I'm smoking too much and not working but
feeling fine

Poem Beginning With A Line From Paul Eluard

putting another day in the world
a little bit of hair comes out
the elder Hieronymous now lives in Denver
he made it sound, I don't know, demeaning
if you don't get your newsletter you should
go to a meeting, shake em up
get what you can from good company
the strong light
on the polished metal pieces

Plenty Of Whiskey

you're a day person I can tell
the black fountain pen seems
correct, elegant
spending a little money calmly
looking for the way to live
the split seconds making me
weightless by surprise
in the bathroom Carol
winds up her hair
tests the water

Pearls

oysters irritated for years to form these
spherical wonders

in THE SCARS OF DRACULA the priest can't go on
so he prays. the young guy straps on the crucifix
like a pistol

I moved your stuff from last night

printing the latest and best in American poetry,
sitting under a tree with a rifle and tuna sandwich,
nothing is stationary
everything wiggles
shots from the south west
all the men in orange hats watch the ridge top

and out in Lafayette the eagle on the police car door
is more like a phoenix, a thunderbird
looking for some wire I found that Carol has
lace in her tool box, I don't know
how'm I supposed to do all these dishes while I'm stoned?

Marc Campbell Kidnaps His Muse

towns with mud and the moon half eaten
I walk through the valley of death
but it doesn't bother me

GLACIER

for Ed Engle

far below the land warps
clouds are a sign that the air is rising
the poles radiate
as if to freeze the world

clouds ARE the weather
the ocean's long memory for hot and cold

in February a bitter wind blows out of China
but the sea stays warm
it sends up visible fingers

varying rings of growth
you have to sample thousands
but the ponderosa is like
the ticking of a clock

and the changes in the sun

if they are real
they are cryptic

coffee
no radio
good health flops over
but there's hope
like the fascination with
horror movies
that after death we can
have a little fun

home from work, standing in the kitchen
the dogs carefully smell my clothes while I
look at the clock, sing, wash
God might wonder at this reaping and sowing,
Charley George (you great booming son-of-a-bitch)
and the American Gas Association

Love Poem

the beautiful towers of mathematics are
like a lonesome duck in the snow
out in the street
Carol starts up her little flesh colored Opel

and I'm happy
sitting in the shop
drinking something to get up
smoking something to stay level
you're like coffee to me baby
I need you to be normal

listing these things
to get at something
the cat on the stuffed mule deer
evening
late evening
total darkness

a moving van stops at the light
no traffic for miles
the van sits
I sit
the furnace comes on
mid March

1 a.m.
light variant
my sister writes;
we see less and less pheasants as more houses are built
getting high
getting late
the fabled streets of Denver
and a great weariness
the cab driver says; "I don't talk to strangers"
the lonely texan settles back
watches the lights, cars
and thinks of springs hanging like spanish moss
under the chairs in Galveston
ah, Texas.
I pace. the dogs follow from room to room
innocent, suspicious

driving
looking up at the darting black spots
(barn swallows)
spending $8 on books
in that dreamlike space between
the last job and the next
the stately wet autumn
the brightly colored children
coming out of the school
I hope the weather stays socked in
whole days with the virtues of evening
a little sad
a little down at the heels

it's hard to believe
some people are so pretty
they go through life like a treasure
you catch a glimpse of red cliff
between the houses and feel a flutter high in the chest
like with too much coffee
the sun outlines the roundness of a pole
and it goes from daylight to lamplight smoothly
with little sadness
and a breeze in the russian olive
saving
savoring
the last cigarette
Talon blue thread, onion seed, glass of pencils
and no music
the traffic is like some natural thing

dust
lightning
a white-faced ibis
and millions of three toed tracks in the mud
like cracks in the fabric of things
the soft spanish walls around the food stamp office
it adds up

double clutching the Ford becomes second nature
the silence of the house in late afternoon
only a dog lapping water
"kitty want a nice ripe sparrow?"

you get into these different tiers of mystery
the workings of your respective jobs
a stretch of wet cold days after an illness
and the sound the cars make
like the sea

in the marsh by
Valmont Rd.
the american
egret next to the great
blue heron
this lake is
patrolled
the sprinkler in the cemetery
has a feeling of gaiety
a good sunset on Saturday night and the fast
chrome and purple Camero full of girls
"I'm going to the flea market is there anything you need?"
ya, a big waste basket for all my mistakes

I think Sundays should be quiet
like a silver Mustang parked on the grass
there's an old fat family counting
gallons of gas and cigarettes towards the grave
while Carol talks on the phone in a green towel
and I am young

a light moves in the school at 6:30 in the morning
just as I look at the bird feeder
the streetlight goes out
ah, light sensitive device
one kid shows up
and there's the impulse to
salvage something
take a big step

Photo: Gil Lipp

About the Author

GIERACH, JOHN, poet; b. Glenwood, Ill., Nov. 24, 1946;
first poems appeared 1964 (in high school); moved, with par-
ents, from Ill. to Minnesota to Ohio; B.A. in philosophy
Findlay College, 1968; after college travelled widely, wrote,
worked alternately as a laborer and musician (was once con-
sidered a fair to middling guitarist); NY, Calif., points be-
tween; has worked as a miner, dishwasher, landscaper, wood
cutter, country club grounds keeper, etc., now drives a garbage
truck; lives in Lyons, Colorado on the banks of the St. Vrain
river; an avid fly fisherman and bird watcher; founder, editor
& printer of Lodestar Press; poems & criticism in small presses;
one previous book: MOTEL THOUGHT IN THE 70s.

CHERRY VALLEY EDITIONS

____ IN MEMORY OF MY FATHER — CHARLES PLYMELL
recording by ROD McKUEN of an elegy for the poet's father.
0-916156-13-3 — LC 76-44678 $ 3.00
signed and lettered by Plymell — 0-916156-11-7   13.00

____ VIBES OF THE SAINTS — PAUL GRILLO — intro.
Claude Pelieu-Washburn — poems and collages
0-916156-10-9 — LC 76-48211   3.50
26 copies signed and lettered by the author including
an original collage — 0-916156-11-7   50.00

____ WHISTLING DOWN THE WIRE — CLAUDE PELIEU -
WASHBURN — translated by MARY BEACH — a new
collection of poems by France's most exciting poet since
Rimbaud. 0-916156-21-4 — LC 77-373   3.50

____ COCA NEON / POLAROID RAINBOW — CLAUDE
PELIEU — translated by MARY BEACH.
0-916156-01-X — LC 75-29324   2.50
signed and lettered — 0-916156-24-9   7.50

____ ELECTRIC BANANA — MARY BEACH — intro.
WILLIAM S. BURROUGHS.
0-916156-07-9 — LC 75-33678   1.50

____ ARE YOU A KID? — CHARLES PLYMELL — a new
collection of poems by the author of THE LAST OF
THE MOCCASINS — these poems were written while
working in the poets-in-the-schools programs during the
last few years. 0-916-156-25-7 — LC 77-12698   3.00
0-916156-28-1 signed and lettered by the author   15.00

____ TALE OF THE AMAZING TRAMP — DAN PROPPER —
"He's a cultural historian and sentimentality isn't there
for its own private weeping self, but as a radioactive
tracer of our times." Hugh Fox
0-916156-22-2 — LC 76-58849   2.50

____ ENERGUMEN — DAN RAPHAEL — "This panorama of
America with black humor captions is Raphael's answer
to the filmaker's montage." ALA Booklist, p. 1332
0-916156-08-7 — LC 75-33132   1.00

____ COBBLE STONE GARDENS — WILLIAM S. BURROUGHS
"Nostalgic glimpses of a young man's boyhood years and
military experiences occasionally penetrate the smoke
screen of spliced sentence fragments characteristic of
Burroughs' cut-up technique." ALA Booklist
0-916156-14-1 — LC 76-40473   3.00

____ LOOKING FOR MINERALS — JOHN BRANDI — Poems
grateful in their loneliness; it is a book of seasons
0-916156-00-1 — LC 75-28076   1.00

____ METAL — JOHN MOULDER
0-916156-05-2 — LC 75-22459   1.00

____ HIROSHIMA FLOWS THROUGH US — BROWN MILLER
The thread of Hiroshima and cancer runs throughout these
poems. Certainly they will become part of the anti-war
literature. Brown Miller has given us a scary picture of the
effects of the bomb on all of us.
0-916156-23-0 — LC 77-22290   2.50
0-916156-29-X — signed and lettered by the author   12.50

FORTHCOMING:

____ THE BLUE AND THE GRAY — JOSHUA NORTON
"It is the ideal bicentennial poem-toast. Edgar Allan Poe
thumbs-a-ride on a neon drenched freeway. The army of
the Potomac protects Saigon. The Salem witches cruise
through Disneyland. A book that takes root and thrives,
in a time of few blossoms." Paul Grillo
0-916156-09-5   2.50

____ JOURNAL OF A HERMIT & — JANINE POMMY VEGA
The first section is a "prose/poem allegory in 22 parts,
which explores what it meant to discover, the monk in all
of us, a trip down a road almost covered now with carbon
monoxide...." William Harrold. The second section con-
sists of love poems and songs, tributes written by this fine
poet during the late 60s and early 70s.
0-916156-30-3 — LC 77-15497   2.50

____ UNDER THE WEIGHT OF THE SKY — KIRK
ROBERTSON — A full length collection by one of the
best small press editors (SCREE and DUCK DOWN
PRESS). 0-916156-22-2 — LC 77-23446   2.50

MAGAZINES:

NORTHEAST RISING SUN — a small press review magazine —
Pamela Beach Plymell — editor.
"Excellent for notes on unusual small press items." Bill Katz
"NORTHEAST RISING SUN is not a song by Bob Dylan."
                                    Publisher's Weekly
Subscription rate: $8.00 per year — single copies $1.50

COLDSPRING JOURNAL — "Brilliantly eccentric" Bill Katz
"The magazine is relatively new, but the spirit is as old as the
little press movement. A must for any self respecting library
with a meaningful interest in modern writing." LJ
single copies: $1.50

TERMS FOR DIRECT ORDERS:

Single copies, no discount, please add 50 cents for shipping.
2-4 copies: 20% discount
5 or more copies: 40% discount
New York State residents please add 6% sales tax.

ORDER FROM: CHERRY VALLEY EDITIONS, Box 303,
             CHERRY VALLEY, NY 13320

$2.50

Cherry Valley Editions
Box 303
Cherry Valley
NY 13320